Mary Queen of Scots

A Mary Queen

of Scots

Biography

Anna Revell

Table of Contents

The Final Years

The Babington Plot

Final Trial

Execution

Legacy

Four hundred years after her death, Mary Stuart, Queen of Scots, is no longer the divisive political figure she once was back in the 16th century. Yet the woman's life continues to be retold today. Whether seen as a romantic tragedy, a frustrating political failure, or a Scottish triumph over British history, Mary's story never fails to fascinate.

Kin and Country

In the mid-16th century, Western Europe was still very much the product of the previous one thousand years of feudalism. While each sovereign state had a recognized system of law and order, these still maintained almost the same medieval political system: hereditary monarchs and their families maintained control over a realm, with the help of powerful lords who had sworn perpetual fealty to the crown and had direct control over portions of the kingdom.

And just as it had been during the Middle Ages, the Roman Catholic religion and the Pope in Rome still held ultimate authority over all. The legitimacy of any monarch's hold over a country was based on his anointing by a local representative of the Catholic Church as its rightful ruler — giving the so-called divine right of kings to rule, under the laws of God and of men.

But challenges to this world order had begun. With Martin Luther and the rise of Protestantism against the Pope's authority in the first half of the 16th century, the people of Europe grew bitterly divided along two camps: those loyal to the Roman Catholic faith, and the Protestants. Soon, this division touched the lords and monarchs of Europe as well.

In their zeal to have their country and favored religion dominate all of Europe, it was common for people to plot the overthrow of a ruler who was not on their side. As a result, religious persecutions sanctioned by threatened monarchs (whether Catholic or Protestant) were an ever-present possibility. Many people, great or small, would lose their lives simply for having the "wrong" faith.

To complicate matters further, this was also a world where men were still the preferred heads-of-state. A king's sons were always first in the line of succession; daughters were the absolute last choice if no other heirs were available. Ruling families often struggled in producing viable male heirs, giving rise to situations where a woman had to ascend a throne. And often, the authority of such female monarchs was questioned or mistrusted by the lords of a realm.

Such was the case with Mary Stuart, Queen of Scots.

The Troubles of Scotland

Mary's parents were Scotland's King James Stewart V and his second French wife, Marie de Guise. While both monarchs were staunch Catholics, they faced a growing Protestant movement within their country. They were also grappling with the challenge of producing and safeguarding heirs, male or female.

King James V's first wife was the sickly Princess Madeleine of France, who turned out to be already stricken with tuberculosis and died just a few weeks after their marriage.

This was also Marie de Guise's second marriage. As the eldest daughter of France's Duke of Guise, she was first married off to

Louis II d'Orleans, Duke of Longueville. Their union produced two sons. But just a few years later, Louis died.

To form an alliance with Catholic-ruled France, King James V of Scotland then asked for the hand of Marie de Guise. Leaving the care of her two sons by Louis with the Orleans family, Marie set off to Scotland and married James.

Marie de Guise was a savvy Queen consort. She successfully won the love of the Scottish people by learning their language, and giving King James two sons (named James and Robert).

But King James V was prone to bouts of paranoia, and given to executing members of the Scottish nobility whom he merely suspected of plotting against him. By 1541, both of his young sons by Marie were dead – allegedly poisoned by the family of one of the nobles he had executed.

James was also prone to infidelity, keeping a string of mistresses who bore him a number of illegitimate children. One of these illegitimate sons would become James Stewart, the first Earl of Moray and supporter of the Scottish Protestant Reformation, who would also play a huge, troubling role in Queen Mary Stuart's life many years later.

Yet, despite all this turmoil, Marie de Guise became pregnant once more with James V's third and final child, who would turn out to be Mary.

Troubles with England

Meanwhile, in the neighboring kingdom of England, King Henry VIII ruled.

England and Scotland had a long history of fighting, conquest and retaliations. King Henry VIII, however, was of the ruling Tudor family, who were actually related to the Stewarts. Many years before, King Henry VIII's own sister, Margaret Tudor, had married the previous King of Scotland (King James IV). James V was their son – making him Henry's nephew.

King Henry was infamous for having had six wives. He was responsible for the creation of a new Christian denomination, the Church of England (with himself as its head), which aided him in his ensuing divorce of his first wife, Catherine of Aragon. For this, he was excommunicated by the Catholic Church. This made him deeply unpopular with the Catholics in England and abroad, including Henry's own nephew, the King James V. So when the King of England expected Scotland to turn completely Protestant as well, his nephew refused.

This infuriated King Henry. It also gave him the pretext for attempting the re-conquest of Scotland, as English kings had done in days of old.

So Henry began sending English troops to invade Scotland. The largest of these battles between English and Scottish forces was at Solway Moss, just at the south of the Scottish border in the English county of Cambria. Though the English soldiers involved numbered only as little as 3,000, they were well-trained and battle-hardened men who managed to overpower the much larger Scottish army (who reportedly numbered about 20,000). Worse, King James V of Scotland could not be present at the battle to rally his men, for he had developed a high fever and had been forced to recover at Falkland Palace instead.

This was a truly humiliating defeat the King James. Already suffering the effects of the fever and complications of his head cold, James retreated to his sick bed, broken and depressed.

A Semi-Charmed Life

Thus, there was considerably less of the joy associated with births when the Queen Marie finally was delivered of a healthy daughter on December 8, 1542, at Linlithgow Palace near Edinburgh. The little infant was baptized as Mary Stewart soon afterward.

Then a few days later, on December 14, 1542, her father King James V died.

Because of his untimely death, his baby daughter Mary had to be crowned Queen of Scotland on December 9, 1543 at Stirling Castle, at the age of nine months old. A lavish miniature coronation outfit was even made especially for her, which included a jewelled satin gown with long sleeves, a velvet mantle, and a train of ermine. She was held upright on the throne by the presiding Lord Chancellor.

The Infant Queen

In the meantime, Scotland was to be ruled by regents on behalf of the baby Mary. But even the transition into the regency was fraught with conflict.

The Protestant Earl of Arran, who was regent until 1554, had a rival in the Catholic Cardinal Beaton. Beaton claimed that King James V left another will, naming him as the proper regent. Marie de Guise managed to solve this problem by having Earl of Arran removed, and succeeded him herself as the next regent.

Meanwhile, England's King Henry VIII was still searching for a way to unite Scotland

and England into one realm, and to break the Scottish alliance with France. Instead of war, this time he thought of marriage. So he proposed that Mary Stewart be betrothed to his own young son and heir, Edward VI. He planned to have Mary brought up as a Protestant in England.

However, Cardinal Beaton began campaigning for a pro-Catholic, pro-French policy, and pressured the Regent Earl of Arran to give up on King Henry's plans. Scottish Parliament also rejected the English marriage treaty, and opted to renew the alliance with France.

This enraged King Henry once more. He then sent English forces to conduct a series of raids on both Scottish and French territory, including the city of Edinburgh, to harass the

Scots into accepting the marriage treaty. (This conflict was later humorously dubbed as the "Rough Wooing" by historians.) He even had some Scottish merchants headed to France intercepted and arrested. King Henry's actions caused so much anger in Scotland that even the Earl of Arran joined Cardinal Beaton's side and converted to Catholicism. This conflict between the English and Scots would continue for years, even after King Henry VIII died on January 28, 1547.

To aid Scotland and renew the old alliance with France, the French King Henry II offered to send French military forces to fight the English, and to have Queen Mary marry his son, the Dauphin Francis II. The Queen Marie and the Earl of Arran agreed to the match, and by July of 1548 the Scottish Parliament ratified the French marriage treaty.

With the marriage agreement in place, King Henry II of France sent a fleet to safely escort a five-year old Queen Mary Stewart from Dumbarton to Brittany. From there, she was brought to live at the French court. Marie de Guise-Stewart remained behind in Scotland to rule as Queen Regent for her daughter.

A French Upbringing

Despite being separated from her beloved mother, Mary's childhood in France was the happiest and most peaceful time of her life.

As a royal ward and future wife of the Dauphin, Mary was educated in the traditional manner of a French princess.

Mary was taught different languages: French, Italian, Latin, Spanish, Greek, and her native Scots. She learned to read and write prose and poetry, to play the lute and virginals, to sing and dance. She also took up needlework, falconry, and horse riding.

And of course, Mary was tutored in religious matters by a Catholic Scottish priest.

In all contemporary accounts, Mary was described as a delightful and charismatic child – auburn-haired, beautiful, graceful, and vivacious. When the young Francis II met her for the first time, they immediately were affectionate towards each other. (He was four years old; she was five.)

She became a favorite of the French court and of King Henry II himself. She was permitted to have her own little court, made up of her governess, Lady Janet Fleming, and other children, which included two of her illegitimate half-brothers, and the so-called "Four Mary's" – young daughters of Scottish noble families (Beaton, Seton, Fleming and Livingston) who each bore the same first name. These girls would end up becoming lifelong companions for Mary Stewart, all the way to the end of her life.

So profound was her formation among the French that Mary permanently adopted the French spelling of her family name. From then on she would be known as "Mary Stuart" or "Marie Stuart."

When she grew into a young woman, Mary was considered to be attractive, eloquent and intelligent. And at a height of 5 feet and 11 inches, she was tall by 16th century standards.

She became a close friend of the Dauphin's sister, Elisabeth de Valois, and had a strong relationship with her maternal grandmother Antoinette de Bourbon (Marie de Guise's mother), who became one of her principal advisors.

The only one at court who was not too fond of Mary was King Henry II's Queen Consort, Catherine de' Medici. Catherine, it was said, was jealous of her husband's fondness for little Mary, and it made her relationship with her future daughter-in-law difficult. This relationship would eventually set the course for Mary's life.

Wife and Widow

On April 4, 1558, the 15-year old Mary Stuart was made to sign a secret agreement that, if she happened to die without producing an heir with the Dauphin Francis II, the crown of Scotland and her claim to the throne of England would be given to the French crown. This was a detail that King Henry II of Frances wanted emphasized. Only then could Mary marry the Dauphin.

Marriage and Power

Weeks later, Mary and Francis were married at Notre Dame Cathedral in Paris. Of Mary's total 13 years in France, her seemingly happy marriage to Francis was its glorious culmination.

Francis II then automatically became the King consort of Scotland, and – as King Henry II proclaimed – the King of England by marriage. The King Henry even went so far as to have the royal arms of England included in the married couple's coat of arms.

All of this was considered either illegal or righteous, depending on which viewpoint of the Protestant-Catholic rivalry was taken.

During this time, only one of the late King Henry VIII of England heirs remained alive: Elizabeth. His son Edward had succeeded him, but died too early; his eldest daughter, Mary ruled afterward but died without producing an heir, as well. Under the 1543 Third Succession Act which the Parliament of England had previously passed, Elizabeth was the next rightful heir. Moreover, King Henry VIII's last will specified that their relatives, the Stuarts, were to be kept from succeeding the English throne. Thus Elizabeth was crowned Queen of England within the same year that Mary and Francis were married.

Yet to many Catholics in and outside of England, Elizabeth was only Henry VIII's bastard child with Anne Boleyn, whose marriage to the Henry was not recognized by the Catholic Church – and therefore, ultimately could not accord Elizabeth the divine right to rule. To these Catholics, Mary Stuart was the only legal Tudor descendant, being the granddaughter of Henry VIII's older sister Margaret Tudor – and therefore, Mary was the rightful Queen of England.

This perennial issue would make Mary Stuart's future dealings with Elizabeth I difficult.

When the elder French king Henry suddenly died in 1559 from injuries sustained in a joust, the 15 year- old Francis and 16 year- old Mary became the new King and Queen of France.

This was Mary's first taste of power as a queen. And with two of her uncles, the Duke of Guise and the Cardinal of Lorraine dominating French politics under her new reign, life was good indeed.

The White Queen

Meanwhile, in Scotland, the Queen Regent Marie de Guise was struggling. The Scottish Protestant lords were becoming more prominent, and the Queen Regent was maintaining control over the realm only with the troops being supplied by France.

By 1560, it became impossible for the French to continue sending support to the beleaguered Queen Regent. There was just too much for the French crown to handle. Scotland's Protestant lords had invited English troops into Scotland to help them secure the growing local Protestant movement, while the Protestant Huguenots of France held an uprising in Amboise.

And so Mary's uncles, the Guise brothers (Duke of Guise and the Cardinal of Lorraine) negotiated for a peace settlement instead.

Settling for peace became even more essential when Mary de Guise suddenly died of illness on June 11, 1560. Thus, at the Treaty of Edinburgh in the following month, France and England agreed to withdraw all their troops from Scotland, and to recognize Queen Elizabeth I's right to rule England.

However, while both countries did indeed withdraw all troops, the proud and grieving 17 year-old Queen Mary Stuart stubbornly refused to ratify the treaty. She had just lost her mother, and viewed the Scottish Protestant lords as rebels and the English throne as hers by right.

More grief came within the same year. On December 5, 1560, just a few days before Mary's 18th birthday, the young King Francis II died from a middle-ear infection (which progressed to a brain abscess).

With the death of her mother and husband, Mary took to wearing all-white mourning garb, earning her the French sobriquet of "La Reine Blanche" or "The White Queen."

But there was barely time for Mary to mope. With Francis II dead, the next King of France was his ten year-old brother Charles IX, and Catherine de' Medici was now the Queen Regent ruling on his behalf. And of course, Catherine did not want to have Mary around.

With political power having shifted out of the Guise family's hands, and her welcome at French court turning cold, Mary Stuart was left with no real reason to linger. The 18-year old widow was still young, full of promise, the reigning Queen of Scotland, and the proclaimed rightful heir to the throne of England. She decided she had a birthright to seize, and made plans to leave for Scotland.

Queen of Scots

On August 14, 1561, Mary Stuart boarded a ship on the port of Calais, one in the fleet of galleys and cargo ships which Scotland sent to take her back the homeland.

The fleet was commanded by high admiral of Scotland, the Earl of Bothwell. At the height of her beauty, the young Queen must have made a lasting impression on him.

With a good wind, the fleet landed at Scotland's port of Leith just five days later. Scottish noblemen and Mary's half-brother Lord James Stewart, Earl of Moray, escorted the Queen of Scotland to Edinburgh. Crowds gathered on the way to cheer her arrival.

Culture clash

Mary Stuart's first home in Edinburgh was Holyrood Palace, which in previous years had been rebuilt by her late father, James V.

The palace was well-suited to Mary's tastes. She at once had it decorated richly with furnishings and ornaments she had brought with her from France or from Mary de Guise's collection. Her private rooms were located in the northwest tower, which included a visitor-receiving chamber, a supper chamber, a dressing area, and a bedchamber. But she also had an extra bath house built for herself, where it was said she bathed in white wine to maintain her creamy complexion. The palace also had a large deer park where she would go hunting.

In the true French fashion she was accustomed to, Mary kept a splendid court. She and its members were dressed elaborately. Most of the household servant staff was French. On her first few nights at the palace, bonfires would blaze as she presided over banquets. Later on, she would host the occasional theatrical costume pageant. Musicians, French singers, and poets played music, sang or recited poetry as she and her guests supped or danced.

It mattered little that the young Queen spoke the Scots language fluently; her worldly and sophisticated French ways scandalized the extremely conservative Protestant Scots.

One particularly fiery and self-righteous Protestant preacher was John Knox, whose hatred of female monarchs was well-known.

(He once issued a written denunciation of them in 1558 called "The First Blast of the Trumpet Against the Monstrous Regiment of Women.") He proclaimed from his pulpit that Queen Mary Stuart had brought to Scotland "sorrow, dolour, darkness, and all impiety." He warned the Scottish Protestant faithful that Holyrood would soon become a brothel, and said that the natural attraction men had for Mary was due to "some enchantment whereby men are bewitched."

Mary actually tried to meet and reason with John Knox, to convince the man of the falseness of his assumptions – and even charged him with treason when he refused to cooperate – but to no avail. Knox was later acquitted and released.

Mary's experience with John Knox was, in a nutshell, how problematic her relationship with the Protestant Scots was, especially with those of the nobility. While she was popular with many of her common subjects, her reign made the Protestants among them fear a possible future attempt to turn Scotland back to the "Papists."

Mary's chosen policy was to try to appease them. She dismissed some of her French servants, and then publicly announced that she would not interfere with Scotland's Protestant religion. She was anxious enough to please her Protestant subjects that she sent as many as 48 Catholic priests to prison for saying Mass in secret within her realm, and impeached the Bishop of Dunkeld for trying to administer Catholic sacraments on Easter of 1561. She even took one-third of confiscated Catholic Church revenues for the Scottish Crown.

But she remained a Roman Catholic and attended Masses in private – which made the Protestants somewhat suspicious of her.

There were more problems beyond the issue of religion. The Scottish nobility of the time were also an unruly lot, prone to lawlessness and violent feuding among themselves.

The First Few Years

Despite these challenges, the first few years of Mary's reign over Scotland went relatively well.

Scottish Catholic nobles expected their young Queen to favor them, but they were disappointed. Mary tolerated religious differences. She kept her powerful Protestant half-brother Lord James Stewart, the Earl of Moray, as her chief advisor, for she knew she needed all the support he and his allies could provide. The rest of her Privy Council were composed of both Protestants and Catholics, such as the Protestant Earls of Argyll and Glencairn, the Protestant Lord Ruthven, and the Catholic Earls of Erroll, Montrose, and Atholl.

Mary even supported the Earl of Moray when he set out to quash a 1562 rebellion in the Highlands led by the country's leading Catholic magnate, the Lord Chancellor Huntly.

Meanwhile, Mary began focusing on her duty as Queen. She needed to maintain powerful foreign alliances and provide an heir to the Scottish throne after herself. She began considering finding a new husband from among European royalty. It was no easy task.

Mary's French uncle, the Cardinal Guise of Lorraine, tried to negotiate for a marriage with the Archduke Charles of Austria without her consent, and was rebuffed. Mary tried to arrange her own marriage to Don Carlos, the son of King Philip II of Spain, but Spanish king refused.

Queen Elizabeth I of England tried to downgrade Mary's efforts at building powerful foreign alliances by offering up the English Protestant Robert Dudley, Earl of Leicester, as a possible husband. (Dudley was actually Elizabeth's personal court favorite and rumored lover.) She even tried to bribe Mary into the deal by saying that, if the Queen of Scots married Dudley, Elizabeth would "proceed to the inquisition of her right and title to be our next cousin and heir" to the English throne.

"Wooing" Elizabeth

Mary refused Elizabeth's offer. She found it insulting that her royal cousin would recommend a man who was Queen of England's rumored cast-off lover and a mere "subject."

More importantly, a marriage to someone like Dudley gave Mary no added advantage in getting what she still wanted the most: the English throne. For even as she sat on the Scottish throne, Mary never relinquished her claim as the true heir to the crown of England.

This earned her Elizabeth's lasting mistrust and hostility. Ironically, though, during the early years of both monarchs' reigns their letters to one another were ostensibly friendly and brimming over with goodwill. They would write elaborate declarations of filial love and send little tokens. Elizabeth once even sent Mary a beautiful diamond ring; Mary reciprocated by sending her cousin a miniature portrait of herself set in a heart-shaped diamond ring.

What Mary was really doing was a charm offensive, wooing her cousin into liking her enough to declare her as the next heir to the throne of England.

But Elizabeth feared that if she publicly named a potential heir – whether it was Mary, Queen of Scots or anyone else – it would very likely invite conspirators to plot her downfall and replace her with that successor immediately. "If it became known who would succeed me, I would never think myself secure," Elizabeth once said. On the other hand, she also did not want to ruffle the feathers of English Catholics further by rejecting her cousin outright.

So Elizabeth resorted to all sorts of tactics to avoid discussing the issue.

Once, Mary sent William Maitland of Lethington as her ambassador to Elizabeth's court, to present the case for declaring Mary the heir presumptive. With all the skill of a lawyer, Elizabeth gave Maitland a carefully-worded reply that she knew of no other with a better claim to it than Mary. Arrangements were soon made for the two young queens to finally meet one another in 1562. Then a month or so away from the appointed time, Elizabeth sent Sir Henry Sidney to the Scottish court to cancel the meeting, giving the religious civil war in France (between the Roman Catholics and the Huguenots) as an excuse.

Mary then sent a more silver-tongued envoy, Sir James Melville, to speak to Elizabeth in September 1564 about the succession.

But Melville proved no match for the English Queen, who verbally "fenced" with him and evaded the topic by peppering him with questions about Mary's famed beauty—her hair color, her skin, her height, anything – and asked him to compare it to hers and decide who was fairer. Thus the ambassador was forced to spend time answering those questions, without ever getting the discussion moving on the issue of the succession.

Elizabeth's avoidance of the issue also helped her concede a little to the advice her chief advisor, William Cecil, the Baron Burghley, had been giving her. Burghley worried about the threat of Catholic Europe coming together to depose Elizabeth and place Mary on the English throne, and the return of Catholic domination in England. He vehemently opposed having the Catholic Mary Stuart as Elizabeth's heir.

Eventually Mary abandoned the charm offensive, realizing that it was useless with Elizabeth surrounded by advisors who were opposed to her. She would have to adopt a wholly different approach to gaining the English crown: marriage.

Passion and Weakness

But as charming, intelligent, and courageous as she was, Mary could also be emotional, impulsive, and reckless. Combined with a bit of political naiveté, it made her a poor judge of men's characters — a deadly handicap for a monarch in search of a new husband or allies. Having spent most of her young life shielded in luxury, Mary had yet to experience the danger and complexity of politics, especially that of Scotland's.

Mary now hit upon the idea of marrying Henry Stewart, England's Earl of Darnley. It seemed like the perfect match. Darnley was actually Mary's English-born first cousin, who also had a claim to both the Scottish and English thrones. Darnley's mother was Margaret Douglas, the Countess of Lennox, who was the daughter of Margaret Tudor (English King Henry VIII's sister) by her second husband, Archibald Douglas, the Earl of Angus.

In addition, Darnley's father was Matthew Stewart, the Earl of Lennox, who was also of the ruling Stewart family and third in line to the Scottish throne.

Marrying Darnley would thus strengthen Mary's own claims to both thrones – and that of her future son's. Most importantly, Darnley was Catholic. A Catholic royal couple of this calibre on the Scottish throne was all the more likely to attract the support of England's enemies, France and Spain.

Mary had actually met Darnley earlier in France, back in February 1561, when she was still mourning the death of her husband, the Dauphin Francis. Darnley had been sent there by his ambitious parents, to officially offer their condolences while maneuvering for a future marriage for their son and the newly-widowed Mary.

Their ploy worked. When Darnley was sent to Scotland again, he met Mary Stuart in February 1565 during a visit to Wemyss Castle, and the Queen of Scots fell madly in love with him. To Mary, he was handsome and the "best proportioned long man" she had ever seen – he was over six feet tall. And she was not afraid to show her desire for him.

She doted on Darnley so much that it scandalized the conservative Scots and surprised visiting English diplomats.

Sir Nicholas Throckmorton, the English ambassador who visited the Scottish court in May 1565, wrote that he found Mary so "seized with love in ferventer passions than is comely for any mean personage." On his first audience with the besotted Queen of Scots, he tried to convince her not to hastily confer a Scots peerage on Darnley but failed; she gave it to her lover within the same day.

Queen Elizabeth and member of the Privy Council sent an official request to Queen Mary to send Darnley back home to England immediately, but the Scottish Queen paid no mind to them.

Their courtship was stunningly brief. By July of 1565, Queen Mary Stuart married Lord Darnley at Holyrood Palace, making him King consort of Scotland. Mary had been so eager to marry him that the Papal dispensation allowing the two Catholic cousins to marry had not even been obtained.

The union enraged Queen Elizabeth; she saw her two cousins' marriage as an aggressive move on their part to strengthen their claim on the English throne against hers.

Troublesome Marriage

But for the time being, Elizabeth's anger was the least of Mary's problems. Her quick marriage to Darnley would bring bigger ones.

As soon as they were married, Darnley revealed his true nature. He was often inebriated and was prone to committing marital infidelities. He was vicious and power-hungry, and he deeply resented the fact that he was made only a King consort, sans full political power that his wife wielded. He would prove difficult for Mary to control, and made her life miserable.

Soon, even the English ambassador to Scotland Thomas Randolph remarked in his reports to Queen Elizabeth: "I know now for certain that this Queen repenteth her marriage; that she hateth him [Darnley] and all his kin... She is now so much altered from what she lately was, that who now beholds her does not think her the same. Her Majesty is laid aside – her wits not what they were – her beauty another than it was; her cheer and countenance changed into I know not what. A woman more to be pitied than ever I saw..."

Many of the Scottish nobles were also infuriated by the crowning of Darnley. They abhorred him. To them, he was a beardless effete and useless drunkard who would go into violent fits of rage. Moreover, Darnley's marriage to Mary diminished the political stature of the Protestant branch of the Stuart family – led by Mary's own half-brother and highest advisor, James Stewart, the Earl of Moray.

The Earl of Moray was so displeased that, just a month after the marriage, he and other Protestant lords, including Lords Argyll and Glencairn of the Privy Council, went into open rebellion against Queen Mary. He and the rebels gathered at Ayrshire.

Queen Mary gathered her forces and marched out of Holyrood Palace towards Linlithgow and Stirling, to confront them. Moray then set out to capture Edinburgh, but failed to take the castle. After raising more troops from Edinburgh, with the restoration and support of Lord Huntly and his son, and James Hepburn the Earl of Bothwell, Mary's forces famously tried chasing her half-brother and his rebel lords all around Scotland, but failed to ever engage one another in combat. (The whole affair was nicknamed the "Chaseabout Raid.")

But Moray was unable to gain additional support for his rebellion. By October of the same year, he fled Scotland to gain asylum in England.

Her brother's rebellion quelled, Mary then broadened her Privy Council, replacing the absent rebels with both Catholics and Protestants, such as the Bishop of Ross John Lesley, the Provost of Edinburgh Simon Preston, the Bishop of Galloway Alexander Gordon, and Sir James Balfour.

Pregnancy

Then in October 1565 came the biggest news of all: Mary was with child. This was the prize she had set out to win all along. A Catholic child by Darnley, especially a male heir, would strengthen her hold over the Scottish throne and the Stuart claim to the English crown, and garner international Catholic support for her cause.

But Mary's pregnancy deteriorated her relationship with Darnley even further.

Darnley became more arrogant. He suddenly realized that it would be his son, and not he, who would one day become the anointed king of both Scotland and England. He began demanding the Crown Matrimonial or the right to be co-sovereign of Scotland and keep the Scottish throne if his wife died. But Mary refused.

Darnley also began to suspect that the child was not his at all. There were rumors floating around that Mary's favorite courtier, David Rizzio, was the baby's actual father.

David Rizzio was a young Italian musician whom Queen Mary had appointed foreign secretary. He had inveigled himself into Mary's good graces so well that even senior members of the Privy Council had to go through him in order to discuss state matters with the Queen. The Scottish nobility perceived him as arrogant, and detested the fact that he was a Catholic foreigner, thinking he could very likely be a Papal spy.

Jealous of Rizzio's influence over his wife, Darnley began plotting against him.

Dark Days

The discontent among Mary's nobles about Rizzio's power was so great that, by the first few days of March 1566, despite their religious differences, Darnley managed to conspire with some Protestant lords and gave them his consent to get rid of Rizzio. Ironically, some of these nobles even included those who had previously rebelled against Mary and Darnley's marriage.

The Murder of Rizzio

On the early evening of March 9, a group of lords accompanied by Lord Ruthven and Darnley himself overpowered the royal guards at Holyrood, took control of the palace, and stormed into the private dining room where Rizzio was with the pregnant Queen Mary.

They demanded that Rizzio be handed over to them. When Mary refused and Rizzio hid behind her, they grabbed him. Some accounts say they took Rizzio away before harming him; others say they went ahead and killed him in front of the Queen. Whichever the case, they stabbed him several times till he died.

The tumult within Holyrood roused the Provost of Edinburgh and brought a crowd of armed men to the outer court of the palace. (Darnley was able to dismiss them.) Some accounts say Mary was not able to cry for help, as Darnley and the lords surrounded her and had control of the palace.

They tried reasoning with the understandably distraught Mary so she would accept the assassination.

Meanwhile, Rizzio's body was then dragged down the main stairs, stripped of clothes and jewels, and buried hastily in the Holyrood cemetery a few hours later. (In her grief, Queen Mary would later order that Rizzio's body be interred in the sepulchre of the Kings of Scotland – an extraordinary move which only served to strengthen the rumor that he was her lover.)

The events of the next few days were even stranger.

Mary's half-brother, the Earl of Moray, returned from exile. (Because Queen Elizabeth sympathized with Mary and chastised Moray for having rebelled against the Queen of Scotland; she would not grant him asylum.) Whether or not she believed him to have been involved in the murder of Rizzio, Mary received him once again to her side.

Meanwhile, the lords involved in Rizzio's murder lingered on at Holyrood and continued the pressure on the young Queen, drafting articles for her to sign that guaranteed their security from punishment. But Mary left the security articles unsigned. They at first tried to get assurances from Darnley, as King consort, to keep the Queen under control. But they soon realized they could not trust him,

The return of the powerful Earl of Moray, and the natural mistrust between him and the Scottish lords, must have made Darnley panic. When Mary tried to convince her husband that siding with the Protestant Scots was politically dangerous, he regretted his involvement in the murder and switched sides.

On the night of March 11, with the help of the captain of the palace guards, and the Earls of Huntly and Bothwell, she and Darnley escaped the conspirators at Holyrood Palace via the underground passages in the chapel of the royal tombs. Then they headed off for the safety of Dunbar Castle.

Their escape to Dunbar caused the other conspirators in Rizzio murder to flee Holyrood. Mary and Darnley were able to return to Edinburgh on March 18.

Regaining control over her government, Mary pardoned her brother Lord Moray, and the Lords Argyll and Glencairn for their involvement in the previous Roundabout Raid rebellion, and restored them to the Privy Council. She even pardoned her husband Darnley for the murder.

But she also cleverly convinced her King consort to issue a public proclamation of his innocence in the matter. He foolishly complied.

His proclamation, published at Edinburgh, denied his involvement in the Rizzio murder, and called his fellow accomplices backbiters and slanderers for claiming he was. He declared upon his honor that he never had "any part of the said treasonable conspiracy," nor "counselled, commanded, consented, assisted, or approved the same."

In reply, the betrayed conspirators sent Queen Mary copies of the bonds Darnley had signed for Rizzio's murder. Mary now had written proof of his treachery.

The Birth of James VI

But for the moment, there was something more pressing for Mary to prepare for: the birth of her son.

She retreated to Edinburgh Castle to prepare for it. On June 19, 1566, after a long and painful labor, she gave birth to James VI of Scotland, between ten and eleven in the morning. The baby was strong and healthy.

Weakened as she was by the stressful events that preceded the birth, Mary kept up the appearance of reconciliation. It must have been difficult, for she had brought herself into a strange and dangerous political situation. She loathed her husband. Her best advisor was her brother, the Lord Moray, who still held some hostility towards her for having married Darnley. And it was only with the help of Lord Moray and a few other lords that she held her noblemen in check, as half of them were also hostile toward her or could not be trusted because they had previously rebelled against her.

What she had truly planned to do with her troublesome husband though, remain shrouded in mystery. The surviving accounts differ as to what Queen Mary really meant to do.

It was at this point that Mary seemed to have decided to put all her trust in James Hepburn, the Earl of Bothwell. To her, Bothwell was a faithful ally who had previously served her mother Marie de Guise. He had safely ferried Mary from France to Scotland at the start of her reign, and later helped her escape the Rizzio conspirators at Holyrood.

It was said that this was the point where her trust and admiration for Bothwell turned into love. Others said the feeling was mutual, and that Bothwell had his own future designs for the Queen of Scots.

Toward the end of November 1566, Mary met with her lords at Craigmillar Castle to discuss her problem with Darnley. The subject of divorce was taken up, but nothing more than that was explicitly mentioned between the Queen and the nobles.

Darnley Falls Ill

Upon hearing of the meeting, Darnley feared for his own life. He then planned to flee to France. He waited until after the Catholic baptism of the infant James VI at Stirling Castle shortly before Christmas 1566 to make his escape.

But at the start of his journey, Darnley was stricken with fever. (It was said it was possibly due to syphilis or smallpox.) He only got as far as Glasgow, where he decided to convalesce at one of his father's estates.

When Mary heard of this, she journeyed to Glasgow and, like a loving wife, attended to Darnley at his sickbed. She helped him rest and recover, and even spoke to him about reconciliation.

By late January 1567, Darnley was feeling better, but still recuperating from his illness. Mary then asked him to move to Edinburgh so he could be closer to where she held court, so she could more easily visit him. He complied, and continued his recuperation at a house that belonged to a brother of Sir James Balfour, located at the former abbey of Kirk o'Field, near the Edinburgh city wall.

Mary would pay her husband long visits every day, so it did appear that reconciliation was possible. But in the evening of February 9, 1567, Mary visited him only for a few hours, before returning at once to Holyrood by eleven o'clock to attend the ball and banquet held in honor of the upcoming weddings of her servants, Bastian Pagez and John Stewart.

Darnley's Assassination

At two in the morning, the sound of a huge explosion shook the whole of Edinburgh. It was followed by the sound of falling masonry and the terrified cries of awakened people.

The house at Kirk o'Field was completely demolished by the explosion, and Darnley was dead. Investigators discovered that gunpowder had filled the chamber below Darnley's rooms. Oddly, Darnley's half-naked body was found out in the garden, away from the house. Apparently he had not been blown to pieces by the explosion, but died by some other means, probably by smothering or strangulation. (Though there were no reported visible marks of violence on the body.)

No matter how despised Darnley was while living, the murder of any king was still considered the worst crime in all of Christendom, by Catholic or Protestant standards. People immediately suspected Moray, Secretary Maitland, and the Earl of Morton were involved, but the greatest suspicion fell on the Earl of Bothwell and Queen Mary herself.

Genuinely alarmed at how public opinion was turning against her cousin, Elizabeth wrote to Mary on April 8, 1567: "For God's sake, Madam, act in this case, which so nearly concerns you, with such sincerity and prudence, that all the world may have reason to acquit you of so enormous a crime; for if this were not done, you would justly be erased from the rank of Princes, and be covered with infamy by all the world..."

By the end of February, the rumors led Darnley's grieving father Matthew Stewart, the Earl of Lennox, to demand that Bothwell be brought to trial before the Scottish Parliament. Queen Mary agreed to it. But when Lennox asked for more time to gather evidence, the trial was commenced without his presence, and Bothwell was acquitted of the crime by April 12, 1567.

But tongues continued to wag all over Scotland and the rest of Europe.

With all the stress from Darnley's death, and the nursing of her newborn son, Mary's health deteriorated. For safety, and for her own health, she kept her son at Stirling Castle, while she travelled to and fro Holyrood and other places (such as Seton).

Bothwell's Move

The accounts on the events that follow Bothwell's acquittal are also tainted with conjectures.

According to somewhat hazy intelligence reports gathered for Queen Elizabeth's secretary of state, Lord Burghley, Bothwell invited over two dozen of the most important lords and spiritual leaders of Scotland to meet him at a tavern in Edinburgh. There, he allegedly got them to sign a written bond to support his bid to marry Queen Mary; the Queen had supposedly even signed a warrant authorizing the Lords to enter that bond. Strangely enough, the signers of the bond reportedly included even the Queen's brother, the Earl of Moray.

It was said that Bothwell succeeded in doing all this either by getting the lords drunk, bribing them, or by threatening them the presence of 200 of his own men surrounding the tavern, ready to kill when ordered. Another story says that some of the lords were sincere supporters, while the others agreed because they were planning to use Bothwell's personal ambition to destroy Queen Mary's political standing – giving credence to the version of the story where Mary was entirely innocent of the whole Bothwell affair.

Whatever did truly happen between Bothwell and the lords, what happened next truly did ruin Mary's public reputation beyond repair.

Between April 21 to 23 of 1567, Mary visited her ten-month old son at Stirling – for what would turn out to be the last time. Then, on her way back to Edinburgh on April 24,

Mary was waylaid and abducted by
Bothwell and his men.

Some said she was kidnapped. Others
claimed it was all for show, and that she was
more than willing to go along with Bothwell.

Whichever the case, Mary was brought to
Dunbar Castle, where she stayed – or was
kept – for over a week.

A Curious Choice

Some accounts say that, while at Dunbar,
Bothwell tried to persuade Mary into
marrying him. In a letter she sent much later
to the Bishop of Dunblane, Mary herself
claimed that this was the first occasion
Bothwell ever decided to pay suit to her, that
she rejected him outright. In this version of

the story, Mary eventually relented after much pressure, somehow not realizing that marrying Bothwell would be political suicide.

Others say Bothwell even raped her so she would be forced to marry him, to save her honor. And others say it was all a ruse, to make it appear she was talked into it, when in fact she had planned to marry Bothwell all along by having Darnley assassinated. While Mary was stayed at Dunbar Castle, Bothwell finalized his divorce from his wife, Jean Gordon. (Bothwell was a Protestant.)

Whatever their true motives were, on May 6, Queen Mary and Bothwell returned to Edinburgh. And on the late evening of May 14, they were hastily married at Holyrood, in a Protestant ceremony. Bothwell was made

Duke of Orkney. Only a few people attended the proceedings.

The news quickly spread. Needless to say, all of Scotland and Europe, Catholic or Protestant, were bewildered and shocked by Mary's midnight marriage. It proved a far more unpopular decision on Mary's part than her previous marriage. If she were abducted against her will, they thought, why did she not have him arrested upon their return to Edinburgh? To many, this was proof that she had Darnley assassinated in order to replace him with another husband.

Capture and Imprisonment

Mary believed at first that her Scottish nobles would support her decision. But soon they grew jealous and discontented at the Bothwell's newfound power.

On June 15, twenty-six of the Scottish peers turned against the new royal couple and raised an army, which Mary and Bothwell's forces confronted at Carberry Hill.

But no battle occurred. To prevent bloodshed and to save Bothwell's life, Mary negotiated with the Scottish lords. During negotiations, Mary's own troops grew discouraged and deserted her. However, she was able to secure safe passage for Bothwell from the field – in exchange for her own surrender to lords.

Bothwell thus escaped the scene. He fled Scotland and eventually went into exile in Norway. (He would later die at Dragsholm

Castle in 1578, locked up by the King of Denmark.)

The lords then took Mary back to Edinburgh as their prisoner.

Dressed in ordinary clothes now, the captive Mary was paraded through the streets of Edinburgh as a crowd of spectators roared and howled, denouncing her as a whore, an adulteress, and a murderer. Some accounts say Mary was shocked at the mob's behaviour; it seemed she had not realized how far her reputation had fallen until that moment.

The following day, she was incarcerated at Loch Leven Castle, and placed under the care of the castle's owner, Sir William Douglas.

News of Mary's incarceration reached Queen Elizabeth. She wrote to her cousin on June 23, 1567, and gave both chastisement and support: "...how could a worse choice be made for your honor than in such haste to marry such a subject, who besides other and notorious lacks, public fame hath charged with the murder of your late husband... And with what peril have you married him that hath another lawful wife alive?" Elizabeth goes on to write: "For which purpose we are determined to send with all speed one of our own trusty servants, not only to understand your state but also thereupon so to deal with your nobility and people as they shall find you not to lack our friendship and power for the preservation of your honor in quietness." (The servant Elizabeth was referring to was one of her ambassadors, who brought her letter through to Scotland.)

Meanwhile, the Scottish lords used the whole situation to accuse Mary (and the absent Bothwell) of the murder of Darnley, and of adultery – and thus declared them both unfit to rule the kingdom.

There are stories that say Mary was discovered to be already pregnant with twins – fathered either by Darnley or Bothwell – while she was at Loch Leven, but had a miscarriage sometime between July 20 to 23.

And so on July 24, 1567, while she was in a physically weakened state, the Scottish lords forced Mary to sign the papers of abdication in favor of her baby son James VI, with her half-brother the Earl of Moray as regent.

She had ensured that her son would be King of Scotland, but she would never see him again.

Escape and Exile

After she abdicated, the lords continued to keep Mary at Loch Leven. Stripped of her power and left in peace, Mary's health began to improve. She was still under the care and watchful eye of Sir William Douglas, but was allowed to write and receive letters. She began making plans.

Last Effort

At this point, Mary still had a few options left to her. Her abdication had not been completely accepted by all of Scotland. Even among the Protestants, there were a few lords and subjects still sympathetic to her cause who thought the forced abdication of the Queen was treason.

Her safest option was to go into exile in France, where she could live with her Guise relatives and cultivate the sympathy of the King of France, who would have gladly used her to gain both the Scottish and English thrones.

Still another – much riskier – option would be for her to stay in Scotland, take control over strategic fortresses, and recapture Scotland by degrees until the rebellion was crushed.

Both options required her escape from Loch Leven.

Mary chose to riskier option. First, she gained the sympathy of George Douglas, the brother of Loch Leven Castle's owner. By May 2, 1568, he eventually helped her escape the castle by smuggling her out dressed as a servant girl. She was then rowed across the loch to a waiting group of loyal Scottish lords, who took her to safety.

The Earl of Argyll was among her supporters. Within a few days, a bond was drawn up for Mary's restitution, which was signed by eight earls, eighteen lords, nine bishops, twelve abbots and nearly a hundred barons. Soon, Argyll and the other lords managed to raise an army of about 6,000 men.

The plan was for her and that army to head over to Dumbarton Castle, which was held by another loyal nobleman, Lord John Fleming. From that nearly impregnable position, she could then easily gather reinforcements from other loyal factions, and gradually work her way to regaining control over the entire country.

Final Turning Point

But on Mary 13, while Mary's troops were en route to Dumbarton, Moray's forces were able to head them off and engage them at Langside. Despite Mary's superior numbers, Moray broke their ranks. It was utter defeat. A hundred of the Queen's men were killed, and three hundred more were taken captive.

Mary and her remaining escorts fled. At first they tried to ride further for Dumbarton Castle, but then turned south instead to spend the night at Dundrennan Abbey.

Whatever state of mind Mary was in at that time, she must have thought that the only option left to her now was to ask the support of Queen Elizabeth of England. Perhaps Elizabeth's previous letters had led Mary to think her cousin would receive her cordially and provide her the means to retake Scotland.

The following morning, she made the decision to begin her journey further south into England. She would never see the shores of Scotland again.

On May 16, 1568, with an escort of twenty companions, she crossed the Solway Firth and into Workington in England's northern county of Cumberland.

Arrest in England

Mary's arrival at Workington caused such a stir among the English border officials that they argued over what to do with her. Mary spent the night at Workington Hall while they sorted it out. From there, she wrote a letter to Queen Elizabeth, informing her where she was.

The next day, Mary and her companions moved further inland to Cockermouth. There, on May 18, 1568, she was met by Richard Lowther, the deputy of Lord Scrope of Carlisle Castle, who escorted her there for protective custody.

Meanwhile, the Earl of Northumberland, under whose jurisdiction Workington fell, also received a letter of authority from the Council of the North – under Lord Burghley's direct orders, apparently – that bid him to "let none of them escape."

Queen Elizabeth proved not to be Mary's ally, but her cautious jailer. Because the

Catholic Queen of Scots had laid claim to the English throne numerous times in the past, she was a natural magnet for forces plotting to depose the Protestant Queen Elizabeth from her throne. So while Elizabeth did not want her cousin dead, she did not want Mary running loose within her own realm or elsewhere.

Elizabeth's solution was to keep Mary under indefinite house arrest.

The Exiled Queen

To prevent England's enemies from colluding with Mary for any plots to overthrow the Protestant "pretender," Elizabeth made it her policy to move Mary from castle to castle.

At first, Mary's "confinement" was far from an oppressive imprisonment. Though Mary's movements were limited and under the constant watch and strict supervision of English officials and staff (handpicked by Lord Burghley for their loyalty to the English crown), she was allowed to hold her own small court of knights, servants and ladies-in-waiting.

When Carlisle Castle proved unsuitable for keeping Mary, by mid-July of 1568 she was transferred to Bolton Castle, another fortress under Lord Scrope's keeping.

There, she was even given Henry Scrope's own apartments at the South-West tower to live in. Mary's chambers were also decorated with her cloth of state, which famously had the French phrase *"En ma fin est mon commencement* (In my end lies my beginning)," embroidered on it.

Around 30 of her men and six ladies-in-waiting were able to stay with her in the castle, while the rest of her retinue took up lodgings nearby. Her household staff included cooks, grooms, a hairdresser, an embroiderer, and a medical team (apothecary, physician, and surgeon). To make Bolton Castle more suitable for the Queen of Scots, furniture, rugs, and tapestries were borrowed from nearby Barnard Castle and other local houses.

While at Bolton, Mary was even allowed to wander the surrounding lands and go hunting. For her health, she was allowed to visit the spa town of Buxton. There was plenty of leisure time. She spent much of her time doing embroidery. She struck up a friendship with one of Queen Elizabeth's courtiers, Sir Francis Knollys, who tried to teach her the English language and convert her to the Protestant faith. She was even allowed, on occasion, to receive Catholic visitors.

Mary also wrote regularly to Elizabeth, protesting against her confinement in England. She would ask if they meet face-to-face. But Elizabeth would demur, saying that it was politically risqué for the Queen of England to be seen with the Queen of Scots while she had not yet been acquitted of her involvement in the murder of Darnley.

The Casket Letters

Queen Elizabeth caused an official inquiry (called the Conference at York, Westminster, and Hampton Court) into Mary's case, which was held from October 1568 to January 1569. Though Elizabeth forbade Mary's attendance in the conference, Mary refused to do so anyway, outraged that an anointed sovereign such as herself would face such an inquiry.

Scotland's Regent, the Earl of Moray, had the so-called "casket letters" presented at the conference as incriminating evidence of Mary and Bothwell's adultery and guilt in Darnley's murder. These were love letters allegedly written by Mary to Bothwell, marriage contracts, and sonnets that were found in a silver-gilt casket that purportedly belonged to Mary. (It bore the monogram of the late King Francis II of France.)

While the authenticity of these letters is disputed today, the majority of the commission of the inquiry (including the chair, the Duke of Norfolk), considered them likely genuine. But Queen Elizabeth then declared that the evidence was insufficient, proving nothing against Mary or the confederate lords now ruling Scotland.

This was precisely the political exercise Elizabeth needed to keep the entire situation the way she wanted. Elizabeth's advisors constantly worried over the political threat Mary's presence posed to the realm, while Elizabeth herself refused to do anything drastic regarding Mary's fate – she wanted no anointed sovereign's blood on her hands. Thus, the commission gave her the license to keep the status quo: a Protestant government in Scotland with a Stuart king on the throne, without ever having to release or condemn Mary.

Elizabeth then decided her cousin had to be more closely monitored. In January 1569, Mary was transferred from Bolton to the decidedly less comfortable Tutbury Castle in Staffordshire, under the custody of the Earl of Shewsbury.

Limbo

Thus Mary remained confined under the watchful eye of the English crown, over the next 19 years. Occasionally she was moved from one castle to the next castle.

In Scotland, Mary's supporters continued a civil war in defense of her rule, before they lost the fight in 1573, after English troops were sent to Scotland to help. (The arrival of

English troops were triggered by the assassination of the Earl of Moray in January 1570.)

Over those years, a few English throne-takeover plots were also made in Mary Stuart's name – like the Ridolfi Plot (1571) and William Parry's assassination attempt on Elizabeth (1585). Such plots would prompt Mary's removal from one castle to another.

Mary's health steadily had been steadily going in a decline during her confinement, due to lack of exercise and the increasingly Spartan conditions of her living conditions. (Tutbury Castle was cold and damp.) By the 1580s she had difficulty walking due to severe rheumatism. Also during this time, Mary's son, James VI of Scotland, came of age and assumed the throne of Scotland at the age of 15. (He was, of course, raised as a Protestant.)

In 1584, a few years into James' reign, Mary sent a proposal to her estranged son that she hoped could alleviate the conditions of her captivity. She was willing to stay in England and abandon her bid for the English throne, to grant general amnesty for the Scottish lords, and agree that Elizabeth would have a say in any future marriage arrangements James would enter. Most importantly, she agreed there would be no change in Scotland's predominantly Protestant religion. All this she proposed, exchange for some liberty in exile.

But her son James rejected her proposal and instead signed an alliance treaty with Queen

Elizabeth – in effect, abandoning his mother to her fate, for the sake of political gain.

The Final Years

During Mary's imprisonment in England, the persecution of Catholics continued under Queen Elizabeth. Catholics were forced to practice their faith in private, while appearing outwardly Protestant. Catholic priests caught traveling incognito in England could be arrested and imprisoned. Anyone caught saying or attending Mass, even in private, could be sentenced to death. But all this seemed to only fan the ardour of some Catholics for the cause of Mary, Queen of Scots.

In 1584, Queen Elizabeth's Privy Council signed the "Bond of Association" that deemed any plot made against the Queen of England, in the name of anyone within the line of succession – whether instigated by that heir or not – could be tried for treason and executed.

Lord Burghley and Sir Francis Walsingham, England's Secretary of State, were anxious to use this law and remove the Mary Stuart problem once and for all. So they decided to lay a trap.

The Babington Plot

In 1585, due in part to ill health, Mary Stuart was transferred from Tutbury to Chartley Hall, a moated and battlemented mansion. But she was also placed under heavy guard and strict confinement, under the watch of Sir Amias Paulet, a Puritan loyal to Queen Elizabeth.

Walsingham then employed double agents. The agents infiltrated the network of English Catholic conspirators that included Anthony Babington and John Ballard, who were planning to free Mary Stuart from captivity and assassinate Queen Elizabeth. After achieving these, their goal was to have Mary as Queen of England, and have England overrun and restored to the Catholic faith with the invasion of the Catholic League in France and the forces of Spain's King Philip II.

Babington then began sending secret letters to Mary at Chartley Hall, asking for her advice and support. The letters and Mary's subsequent replies were hidden inside a watertight casing, within the stopper of a beer barrel that was part regular provisions sent to the castle. All the secrecy was in vain, of course, because Walsingham's double agents were part of the chain of communication between Mary and the conspirators.

Unfortunately for Mary, she suspected nothing. She wrote her replies to Babington and his accomplices, giving advice on how to do a successful rescue, and of the need to assassinate Elizabeth.

Walsingham had the proof he needed of Mary's intent and involvement.

Final Trial

On August 11, 1586, while she was out riding, Mary was arrested and held at Tixall Gatehouse. Then she was moved to Fotheringhay Castle, which would be her final prison.

In October, she was finally put on trial for treason at the great hall in Fotheringhay before a court of noblemen (which included Lord Burghley and Walsingham). No matter how Mary courageously she defended herself, criticized the legality of the proceedings, and denied the charges, the court was determined to convict her. And so she was sentenced to death on October 25.

She exhorted the men of the court to "remember that the theater of the whole world is wider than the kingdom of England."

Despite the sentence, Queen Elizabeth hesitated in pushing through with Mary's execution. Elizabeth worried about the consequences, especially concerning what Mary's son, James VI, would think. So Mary remained imprisoned at Fotheringhay for a few more months, not knowing if she would indeed be executed or not.

But finally, after much pressure from her own Privy Council, Elizabeth signed Mary's death warrant on February 1, 1587.

Accounts of the day are unclear as to what Elizabeth truly intended by signing the warrant. Some say that she merely wanted the document signed and ready for use in case of emergency, and had not intended to have the warrant served. Still others say that Elizabeth mistakenly signed the death warrant without realizing what it was, because it lay on top of a pile of other documents that needed her urgent signature.

On February 3, 1587, Lord Burghley summoned together ten members of the

Privy Council, and they decided to carry out the death warrant at once. Whether Elizabeth knew of their plans or not was not clear. She had purposely been vague and indecisive about the execution, perhaps in an effort to avoid the responsibility for the deed as much as possible.

On February 7, 1587, Mary was told that she would be executed the following day.

Execution

Mary spent the last hours of her life praying, writing her will, writing a letter to the King of France, and distributing the remainder of her belongings to members of her household.

The scaffold was set in Fotheringhay's great hall, and in the middle was the block, a cushion for Mary to kneel.

When the execution ceremony commenced, Mary Stuart walked in dressed in black satin, holding her prayer book and rosary in her hands. When she was made to undress and remove her outer garments, her crimson inner garments were revealed. She had purposely dressed in the color of Catholic martyrdom, determined to make her death remembered as a dramatic, unjust sacrifice for the faith. Her last words were in Latin, *"In manus tuas, Domine, commendo spiritum meum,"* echoing the last words of Jesus Christ at his crucifixion – "Into thy hands, O Lord, I commend my spirit."

Her death was gruesome and pitiful. The executioner's first blow somewhat missed her neck and struck mostly the back of her head. (Some say Mary cried out, "Sweet Jesus!" at that point.) The second blow finally severed the head off the neck, except for a remaining piece of flesh, which the executioner then hacked off with the axe, cleaver-style. Then he held the severed head aloft by the hair, and said for all to hear, "God save the Queen!" – however, Mary had been wearing a wig to hide her graying hair, and the head slipped off the wig and rolled to the ground.

When Queen Elizabeth learned of Mary Stuart's death, she immediately became angry and distraught. She mourned for her cousin's death, and blamed everyone on the Privy Council, claiming they all acted without her authority. She continued to shunt the blame to everyone else but herself, for the rest of her life.

Legacy

Mary Stuart, Queen of Scots is currently interred at Westminster Abbey, not far from where the Tudor half-sisters, Queen Elizabeth I and Queen Mary I, lie.

She had initially been buried in a simple coffin at Peterborough Cathedral, but she was reinterred at Westminster in 1612, upon the orders of her son, King James VI of Scotland, when he became King of England.

For that's precisely what happened when Queen Elizabeth finally died of natural causes in 1603, without having ever married and giving birth to an heir – Mary Stuart's son succeeded her as King James I, being the only rightful heir in the line of succession to the English throne.

And because Scotland's son had become King of England as well, after centuries of turmoil, England and Scotland finally became united as one nation.

Was Mary Stuart a political failure? From a certain perspective, it could be said that Queen Elizabeth of England won in their rivalry; Elizabeth was certainly the more astute politician. But it's Mary Stuart who has won the long-term victory -- her life and death brought Scotland blood to the throne of England, after centuries of resistance from English occupation. Every British monarch from then on carried the blood of Mary, Queen of Scots.

Made in the USA
Middletown, DE
24 December 2018